One Bee

Got on the Bus

Written by Nancy Dowd
Illustrated by Michael Compton

Six bears got on the bus.

Five bunnies got on the bus.

Four butterflies got on the bus.

Three bats got on the bus.

Two bugs got on the bus.

One bee got on the bus.

Buzz!
One bee is on the bus.